How Animals Communicate

How Animals Communicate

Betty Tatham

Franklin Watts
A Division of Scholastic Inc.
New York • Toronto • London • Auckland • Sydney
Mexico City • New Delhi • Hong Kong
Danbury, Connecticut

To our children, Rich and Sue

Note to readers: Definitions for words in **bold** can be found in the Glossary at the back of this book.

Photographs © 2004: Animals Animals: 10 (Don Enger), cover (Johnny Johnson), 25 (Gerard Lacz), 48 (Raymond A. Mendez), 15 (Oxford Scientific Films), 14 (Fritz Prenzel); Corbis Images: 30 (Gallo Images), 45 (Michael Maconachie); Dembinsky Photo Assoc.: 2 (Sharon Cummings), 42 (Marilyn Kazmers), 50 (Skip Moody); Minden Pictures: 5 right, 17 (Jim Brandenburg), 5 left, 20, 21 (Gerry Ellis); Peter Arnold Inc.: 44 (Fred Bavendam), 52 (David Cavagnaro), 13 (Jean-Paul Ferrero/Auscape), 23 (Martin Harvey), 33 (S.J. Krasemann), 41 (Gerard Lacz); Photo Researchers, NY: 37 (Cosmos Blank), 38 (Scott Camazine), 29 (Jeff Lepore), 8 (Maslowski), 6 (Mitch Reardon), 27 (David Schleser); Visuals Unlimited: 46 (Joe McDonald), 18 (David Wrobel).

The photograph on the cover shows a young emperor penguin communicating with an adult emperor penguin. The photograph opposite the title page shows two prairie dogs kissing.

Library of Congress Cataloging-in-Publication Data

Tatham, Betty.
    How Animals Communicate / by Betty Tatham.
        p. cm. — (Watts library)
    Contents: Messages that can be seen—Voice and other sounds—Smell and other chemical signals—Touch tells a story—Animals that miscommunicate.
    Includes bibliographical references and index.
    ISBN 0-531-12167-4 (lib. bdg.)   0-531-16214-1 (pbk.)
    1. Animal communication—Juvenile literature. [1. Animal communication.] I. Title. II. Series.
QL776 .T38 2004
591.59—dc22

2003012576

Contents

A young elephant bull trumpets an angry warning. If it is ignored, he will attack.

Forms of Communication

Groundhogs kiss, elephants trumpet, whales sing, fish drum, bees dance, and skunks spray. These are just a few of the ways animals **communicate**, or tell each other what they want or how they feel. Animals send and respond to messages that are important to them. They use signals that can be seen, heard, smelled, tasted, or touched. Sometimes two or more of the senses are used to give or get a message.

This opossum "plays dead" for the beagle by lying absolutely still. If someone were to roll it over, however, it would flip right back to the "dead" position.

Through its sense of smell, a rabbit knows a coyote is approaching long before it actually sees its enemy. It also hears the coyote race through the underbrush. If the rabbit is quick enough to get to its **burrow** and hide, it may save itself. If not, the coyote's touch will be its last communication with another animal.

Animals communicate for many reasons. One message calls

a family or group together, and another message tells them to run, swim, or fly away and hide. An animal will indicate that it wants other animals to stay away from its **territory** or home ground, that it is looking for a mate, or that it is hunting for a meal.

Animals can give hundreds of messages. Some animals warn others of danger, even at great risk to themselves, while many animals communicate affection to their mate, to their young, to others of the same species, and occasionally to a member of a different species. The larger an animal's brain is, the more complex its communication signals usually are.

Some animals purposely **miscommunicate**, or give a false message, to fool or confuse a **predator** that would want to eat them. Blowfish make themselves look larger than they actually are so they won't be eaten by an enemy, while other animals change color to blend into their surroundings. Opossums are great actors that may get a predator to leave them alone by pretending to be dead.

A pair of western grebes is doing the "rushing ceremony" during courtship. Running on water is also done by males who are competing for a female.

Chapter One

Messages That Can Be Seen

Two western grebes swim next to each other on a lake in Oregon. Suddenly, both birds rise out of the water. Wings flapping and feet thrashing furiously, they run across the water for about 60 feet (18 meters). Later, they dive again and surface, with each bird holding strands of green plant material for nest building in its beak.

The **rushing ceremony**, or running on water, of western grebes also takes place when two males want the same female for a mate. Then, instead of fighting with each other, the two rival grebes race across the water. After the contest, the loser leaves. Sometimes several competing males and a single female perform this ceremony together.

Mating Performance of Other Birds

To attract a mate, male cranes and herons flap their wings in a wild dancing ceremony, while some grouse perform a spiral dance. Albatrosses do a courtship dance together before mating. The male also twists his wings and bows his head. Later, he winds his neck around the neck of the female.

Birds of paradise tumble, somersault, and hang upside down from branches to impress females, while male frigate birds blow up their throat sacs with air, as if they were balloons. This makes them look red. Frigate birds can keep their throat sacs blown up for hours. Courting ospreys may briefly hold each other's claws, with the male flying in the top position and the female hanging down.

Male hummingbirds perform spectacular **display** flights, or shows, to win a mate. They fly in circles, do figure eights,

and **dive-bomb**, flying straight down like a bomb or arrow. They pull up about 1 foot (0.33 m) before hitting the ground. Their brilliant colors sparkle in sunlight and dazzle the plainer-looking female.

The peacock spreads his colorful feathers into a huge fan while he has his back turned toward the peahen. When he suddenly turns around, showing his beautiful colors, he quivers his quills, making a rattling sound. The peahen may then mate with him. Display behaviors are usually done to attract a

The photograph shows a pair of albatross or gooneys during their spectacular courtship dance. Here the male is demonstrating his skills and strength.

A male peacock has fanned his two hundred glittering train feathers into a colorful display to impress a peahen.

mate or to scare off other males. These actions show off the strength, skill, or beauty of the male.

Other Ways to Attract a Mate

When some lizards are ready to mate, they nod their heads, wave their front legs, or walk as if they were marching in a parade. They also change to a bright color or flash a brightly colored throat sac. When an alligator bull wants to mate, he

Bird Mating Behavior

While male birds usually start mating gestures, some female gulls initiate the mating ritual. The female walks over to the male and bumps into his chest, letting him know she is interested in mating.

may stand up on his hind legs, roar, and spray a smelly liquid in front of him to attract a female.

A male wolf spider waves his legs in a special pattern to tell a female that he wants to mate and not be eaten by her. A Cuban male cockroach will raise his wings in a display gesture. If the female bumps him with her **antennae** or her body, that tells him she also wants to mate. In breeding season, the male stickleback fish gets a red belly, erects his fin, and as soon as the female comes near him, swims in a zigzag fashion. She will follow him to the nest he made for her eggs.

The male stickleback fish's red color shows that he is ready to mate.

Warning Signals

Animals may give signals to let others know there is danger. White-tailed deer raise their tails straight up like a flag when they run from danger to tell others to run too. Some scientists suggest that schools of fish are also warned when one fish detects danger and flicks its tail, causing all the others to change direction at the same time.

Gift Giving

A male tern may bring a fish as a gift to the female he wants to mate with. Other birds give pebbles, sticks, or colorful objects they have found to their mates.

A porcupine that senses danger puffs out its quills and raises and shakes its tail. If ready to fight, it will stomp a hind foot, turn around, and run backward, jabbing its quills into the enemy. Before spraying, a skunk will also stomp a hind leg on the ground to warn the enemy to back away. If that doesn't happen, the skunk will quickly turn tail and spray an unpleasant-smelling liquid, causing most animals to run away. Mule deer also stomp a hoof to alert other deer to danger.

An Australian frilled lizard has a ruffled cape around its neck that it puffs out, making it look bigger and more frightening. It also hisses when ready to fight. Blowfish puff themselves up to make themselves look bigger, to discourage enemies from attacking.

Body Language

Wolves have certain behaviors that show whether they want to fight. When a wolf crouches down in front of another wolf with its forelegs stretched out on the ground and its hind legs standing up while turning its head to the side, it communicates

16

that it will be **obedient**. If it walks toward another wolf on stiff legs with its back raised, eyes staring, and teeth showing, that body language says it is ready to fight.

Black-tailed prairie dogs perform a display gesture called jump-yip. An animal throws its forepaws straight up into the air, points its nose up to the sky, and makes a quick, two-part call at the same time. This behavior is used when a prairie dog claims its territory or announces its intention to defend its area from an intruder.

While giving birth, a wildebeest mother and her new pup are both easy prey. To protect them, the herd of wildebeests forms a circle around them, facing outward with teeth bared. This behavior and body language will usually discourage a prowling hyena or other predator from attacking, because the attacking animal doesn't want to fight the whole pack of wildebeests.

A black-tailed prairie dog stands on its home burrow. It is barking to tell others to stay away from its territory.

Learning Sign Language

Dr. Francine Patterson, a research scientist, raised a gorilla named Koko. Dr. Patterson taught Koko to use 375 different signs in American Sign Language by the time Koko was six years old.

Communicating With Color and Light

Grebe chicks have bald spots on top of their heads that are usually yellow, but when they get excited or beg for food, the spots turns red. This lets the parents know when their chicks are hungry.

Damselfish change color and swim up and down quickly when they are looking for a mate. Some fish will turn a brighter color while confidently moving forward, but they turn paler when fleeing from a predator, making it more difficult for the predator to see them. Deep-sea shrimp live in the dark, and their bodies produce greenish yellow, blinking lights that cover their bodies. Usually just one of these lights blinks on at a time. The lights let other shrimp know where they are, making it easier to find a mate. The lights may also communicate danger

This shrimp communicates by blinking tiny lights, one at a time. Many deep-sea animals send messages with colored lights.

and other messages. The blinking on and off of lights on different parts of a shrimp's body may be disorienting to a predator, who can't quite tell where the prey is.

When ready to mate, a male squid flashes waves of neon blue lights over his body. He then spreads his arms wide and strokes the female's head with two forearms until she opens her arms wide and they swim off together. The colored lights are produced by **photophores**, or special cells that glow. The anglerfish has a bony hook over its mouth with a light at the end. This lures prey right into the mouth of the fish when the prey come to investigate the source of the light.

Flying male fireflies flash a signal that is unique to their group. Some species use a code that has flashes close together, while others have a longer pause between the flashes. If a female of the same species wants to mate, she will answer a male's signal from the ground.

Elephant herds communicate with each other over long distances in sounds that are too low for humans to hear. They often "freeze" at the same time—standing absolutely still, ears extended—for as long as a minute to listen for distant calls.

Chapter Two

Voice and Other Sounds

Three groups of fifteen to twenty elephants have been trudging through the desert. For almost a week they have not found any food or water. Some of the young ones have fallen down from weakness, but the mothers and other females make them get up and keep walking. The groups are about 2 miles (3.2 kilometers) apart and they march in silence in the hot sun. Suddenly, all three groups head south and arrive at the same time at a spring, or watering hole, that a scout

A Special Elephant Song

A female elephant carries her calf inside her body for about two years before it is born and then nurses it for two more years. She does not mate during this time. The rest of the time, she is **in heat**, or ready to mate, for three to five days every three months. When the female is in heat, she gives a special call that can be heard by males as far away as 2 miles (3.2 km). The female's song can last half an hour. Usually, there is a fight among the males, and the strongest male will mate with her.

elephant has found. How did the scout communicate that he had found water?

People did not know that elephants communicate by **infrasound** until scientist Katharine Payne proved it in 1984. These sounds are too low for human ears to hear. Only when recordings are adjusted to higher levels can humans hear them. Elephants can hear infrasound from a few miles away because it passes more easily through woods, grasslands, and water than the higher-pitched sounds humans can hear. When an elephant makes these low rumbling infrasound noises, its forehead quivers, showing that the sounds comes from inside the upper part of its nose.

Captive elephants have been observed communicating with infrasound through thick concrete walls by watching the quivering skin on their forehead and recording the low, rumbling sounds that could only be heard by humans after the sounds had been electronically adjusted. Before infrasound communication among elephants was discovered, scientists thought elephants could only trumpet, bark, snort, moan, and growl at levels humans could hear. Recordings of elephant communications for an entire month showed that about two-thirds of the sounds were made at low infrasound levels.

Noises That Carry Messages

Moose and many other animals make lots of noises before mating. They grunt, squeak, and whine. Elk bark loudly when they are ready to fight, while young deer cry like lambs when they want to eat. Beavers communicate that there is danger by slapping their tails on the water's surface. Camels grind their teeth and whip their tails when provoked.

Chimpanzees have many different calls and also communicate by ground slapping, tree drumming, lip smacking, and scratching something. They make one warning call if they spot an eagle, another to warn of a leopard, and a different call to warn of a human. Gorillas are less noisy, but they thump their chests and hoot when they are threatened. Wolves talk to each other with howls, growls, barks, and grunts. A wolf howls alone

A chimpanzee mother makes a loud angry call as she protects her infant from an intruder.

or in a pack. Wolves establish their territory, or home ground, with calls and by leaving scent marks.

Porcupines are especially vocal. They sing alone and with others at mating time. Adults also grunt, whine, cry, and call their mates by clicking their tongues. When threatened, porcupines hiss. Young porcupines mew like cats. They also chatter and shriek.

Sea Mammals Use Sound

Dolphins make more than two thousand different sounds. They talk in clicking or whistling sounds. When bottle-nosed dolphins are anxious or excited, they make a whistling sound. They yelp when they want to mate and bark when there is danger. Dolphins and whales also use sound to determine the location of other animals or objects. They do this by sending out **supersonic sound** or **echolocation** clicks that bounce off objects and return to the sender as an echo, telling it where **prey** or possible predators are located.

Whales also use echolocation to catch prey and to avoid predators. Several whale species sing during mating season, but male humpback whales have the most complex songs. They last up to thirty minutes and are then repeated over and over, often for many hours. Females don't sing, but they communicate with their young with clicking sounds. The beluga whale is also called the "sea canary" because it whistles, squeaks, growls, clicks, mews, and clucks—and sometimes it sounds like a bell.

Call for Help

Oceanographer Jacques Cousteau filmed a sperm whale making mouselike squeaks when it was hurt. This brought other sperm whales to the rescue. They took turns holding it up near the surface so it could breathe.

The bottle-nosed dolphin in front is communicating in clicking sounds we can hear. Its two companions could be sending messages in sounds that are either too high or too low for human ears to pick up.

Whales make clicking sounds by **vibrating** the plug and lip to their **blowhole** as they blow out air. They can whistle at the same time by blowing air through one nostril while making the clicking sound in the other nostril. Sea lions whine, moo, snarl, whistle, grunt, and make short barks.

Birds That Sing

Songbirds sing to attract mates and to establish their territories. Many have different songs or calls, and cardinals have at least twenty-eight songs, while some sparrows have a hundred calls. Most singing is done in the mornings and evenings, and there is more singing in the spring. Some birds sing less often or stop singing while they shed their old feathers and grow new ones.

Emperor penguins in **Antarctica** find each other by voice. After laying an egg, the female sings with her mate and then leaves him to care for the egg for two months. When she returns with food for their chick, the female has to find her mate among thousands of other male penguins. After she recognizes and answers her mate's trumpet call, they call to each other until she reaches him. Their chick whistles to the parents.

Birds have many messages for each other. For instance, blackbirds make a low "chuck-chuck" call to alert others to danger on the ground, and they cry in a high voice if an enemy is in the sky. Crows and many other birds have an assembly call that tells the flock to come together. When a bird is caught by a predator, it gives off a loud, high-pitched cry that warns others of danger. If an osprey is caught, its mate will give off a shrill, loud cry that may startle the predator into dropping its mate. Flying ducks and geese give their position with contact calls. Woodpeckers and flickers communicate by drumming on trees. Because storks have no **voice boxes**, mates greet each other by clapping their bills together many times.

Many Other Animals Also Make Noises

Crickets and grasshoppers also don't have voice boxes. They make their chirping calls by rubbing their wing covers together. Some rub a file that is located on top of one wing against a scraper under the other wing. They may also move their wings up and down while rubbing the file and scraper together. The sound is made louder as it passes through two drumlike structures that are located near the wing covers. These "drum-heads" are made of a bony substance covered by a paper-thin skin that vibrates from the noise. These insects get loudest after dark, when most of them call to attract a mate. Some wood-tunneling insects communicate by knocking their heads against the wooden tunnel walls.

A tree cricket chirps to announce danger. Hundreds of years ago, captured crickets were used as watch dogs in China because they started chirping if an intruder came near.

27

Fooled by Shrimp

During World War II, U.S. soldiers in submarines with earphones picked up the loud clicking noises of shrimp and thought they came from an enemy ship or submarine.

While they lack voice boxes, fish can still be noisy. Some fish make sounds by forcing air from their **swim bladder**, a sac containing air, out of their mouth. Others vibrate their swim bladder using strong muscles. The sea bass pushes its gill covers against bony plates to make a clicking sound when it feels alarmed. The toadfish makes a noise that sounds like a foghorn. Catfish are especially noisy. When they are disturbed, they may hiss, purr, make buzzing or snoring noises, yell, sob, or grunt.

Baby alligators make squeaking sounds when they are getting ready to hatch. Turtles grunt or moan during mating, and some give a loud alarm call when they feel threatened. Some lizards hiss or grunt when they are about to be attacked. Many snakes rattle their tails, and rattlesnakes make a buzzing sound with their tails.

Barnacles attach to rocks at the bottom of the ocean. There, they make clicking sounds that get newly hatched barnacles to float over and attach themselves. Spiny lobsters make grating noises when they rub a ridge at the base of their antennae against the shell on their body. Shrimp make lots of noise when many of them click their claws together.

Some animals stop communicating to avoid danger. Frogs croak or call to attract a mate, but when a nonpoisonous frog sees a bat, it stops calling. It doesn't want to become the bat's next meal. The eastern crow caws an "all's clear" signal whenever it leaves a tree. When it leaves silently, that tells other crows to watch out for danger, and all of them fly away quietly.

The spring peeper frog's loud call for a mate echoes across the water.

Whether a sound message is heard with ears or vibrations are felt with other body parts, sounds help many animals learn about their environments. Animals also use sounds to express their feelings and wants.

This photograph shows a ring-tailed lemur "marking" a young tree by rubbing a strong smelling liquid from a gland near its tail on the bark.

Chapter Three

Smell and Other Chemical Signals

In a clearing in the jungle, two male lemurs, small mammals that resemble monkeys, approach each other, waving their hands, feet, and tails. Each animal has already coated these body parts with a smelly liquid from glands in his chest and wrists. They now paint this strong scent, or smell, on plants around them. Each lemur claims as many places as he can with his own **pheromones**, or smelly chemicals. They also erase each other's smell by rubbing their own scent over a spot that was earlier painted by the opponent. This "stink fight" goes on for about an hour or until one lemur finally gives up and leaves the territory to the winner.

Picking up Smell Signals

Air-breathing animals with backbones receive their pheromone messages through **receptors** located in their noses. As air moves into the nose, scent messages are received and identified by these receptors. Pheromones can travel in liquid as well. Fish pick up smell signals as water moves past their scent receptors. Insects, shellfish, and other animals without backbones can have their scent receptors on different parts of their bodies, including their feet. Smell helps animals find food, avoid danger, discover a mate, locate a place to live, define a territory, and keep track of others in the group.

Some animals use smell to discourage their enemies. Predators avoid skunks because they don't want to be sprayed with the skunks' strong and unpleasant scent. The swallowtail caterpillar's bad smell also keeps its enemies away.

When it is necessary for a group of adult males of a species to live together, such as in a community of captive mice, males may produce special **inhibitor** pheromones that prevent fighting among males that have been living together for some time. The pheromones of females also have this calming effect on aggressive males of some species.

Pheromones at Work

When scientists rubbed the fur of a male mouse with a female's urine before placing the male into a group of strange males, the group of males was only curious but not aggressive toward the newcomer. Without the inhibiting smell, there would have been a fight.

Animals often **bond**, or join together, as a group, by recognizing the pheromones they have in common. When an animal that looks like them but has different pheromones comes near them, they often ignore it or treat it as an enemy.

Marking Territory

Male deer make scratch marks on tree trunks with their antlers and mark their territory by rubbing a gland on their forehead against trees to leave their scent. Rabbits rub glands located under their chins on plants, grass, tree bark, or stones to mark

The buck rubs a gland on his forehead on the bark of a tree. The scent will tell other animals that this is his territory.

their territory. They also leave scent marks from glands on their feet, as do wolves, dogs, coyotes, rabbits, deer, and many other mammals. Bobcats and domestic cats have glands around their mouths and on their foreheads that let them leave their smell on things they rub.

Male wolves and coyotes spend a lot of time marking their territory both by howling and barking and by spraying their urine around the edge of the area they claim as their own. They stop briefly and spray only a few drops at a time, but they spray often. When another male crosses that scent border, he has invaded someone's territory and may be driven off or challenged to a fight. If the invading wolf sprays next to the scent mark of the owner of the territory, he may be saying, "I was here," but if he sprays right on top of the scent mark, it means he wants to challenge the owner for some or all of his territory.

After bears have urinated their pheromones into mud, they roll in the mud. Then they rub their fur on tree trunks to let other bears know that an area is their territory. They also scratch tree trunks with their long claws for the same reason.

Pheromones in Mating Behavior

Many animals produce a special smell when they are ready to mate. This lets members of the opposite sex know where to find them. Some sex pheromones are carried by the air, others by water. Many animals use their sense of smell to find a mate.

When a female crab is ready to mate, she fans her special smell in front of a male's den. After the male crab receives this chemical signal through tiny hairs on his antennae he comes out and invites her in. They must wait until she has shed her hard shell before they can mate. Because of her special smell at this time, the male will not eat her, even though she lacks her tough protective covering.

Sex pheromones released by the body of a female dog are carried by the wind over long distances, and they get a very strong reaction from males that will break a leash or jump high fences to race over to mate. Wild dogs in Africa live in packs, and each group has a dominant male and a dominant female that are mates. To leave a message that these two leaders want to stay together, they jointly mark their territory. When the female stops to spray her territorial mark, the male races after her and flips onto his front legs while aiming his spray at the same patch of grass.

Animals have many ways of sending and receiving mating signals. During mating season, a male moose keeps following a cow moose he wants to mate with. By eating grass on the trail she has dripped pheromones on, he picks up the scent that tells him when the cow becomes willing to mate. By moving his head from side to side as a signal that he also wants to mate, a male tortoise responds to the pheromones of a female that is ready to mate.

Some male butterflies get a female to mate by spraying her

head with a smelly powder. The smell gets her excited and makes her settle down on a plant. Then he dusts her again and they mate.

Finding Food and Water

Pheromones help many animals find food. A snake smells a mouse and follows the trail with its nose, while the mouse smells the snake in the air and races to its hole in the ground. Lions, tigers, and other meat-eating mammals also track their prey through smell. Some hunting animals approach their victim downwind so that the wind is blowing toward the predator instead of blowing the predator's smell to the prey.

Some animals help each other find food or water. Worker ants leave a scent trail to a new food supply for others to find. When elm bark beetles have found a new host tree, they release a scent that calls others of their species to join them. Elephant scouts search for water under the desert sand through smell. When water is found, the scout calls, and elephants from several miles around come to share it.

Many animals without backbones detect scent through antennae that are covered with peg-shaped, hairlike scent receptors. Each receptor has thin walls that have many tiny **pores**, or holes through which pheromones can enter the animal's body. The more receptors there are and the more pores each one has, the stronger the sense of smell will be. A male silkworm moth has about seventeen thousand receptors on

each antenna, and each receptor has about three thousand pores. That means that there are a total of about 50 million holes through which scent pheromones can pass, giving this animal a very keen sense of smell.

Butterflies, moths, houseflies, bees, spiders, lobsters, crabs, and many other animals have some of their scent receptors on their feet. As they walk, they pick up the smell of prey or predators. They clean their feet regularly by rubbing them together.

Having tracked mouse scent, a rattlesnake is now ready to strike.

A honey bee scout is doing a waggle dance to give directions to a new food supply.

Chapter Four

Touch Tells a Story

A scout honeybee returns to her hive with a sample of a new food supply. Worker bees flock around her to learn where they can find this flower nectar. Those closest to her touch one or both of her antennae and can feel every move she makes. In the dark of the hive, the scout bee stands on the honeycomb. Her head points straight up, and then she turns to the left, showing the direction in which the food is located. She dances in a figure-eight pattern on the honeycomb surface as she waggles her head and tail from side to side. After a while, she runs in a straight line that is in the direction of the food. This line goes right through the center of the figure eight in which she has been dancing. Over and over she dances this **waggle dance**, going from figure eight to straight line and back again. Because the food is pretty far away, she dances very quickly, and her wings move quickly, making a whirring sound. The dancer also shares a little of the new food with the bees around her. As soon as they have learned the directions, the worker bees leave the hive, making room for others to touch the scout bee's antennae and learn from her.

Once outside the hive, the bees face the sun and then turn to the left and fly off. They land in a field of daisies that is more than 1 mile (1.6 km) away and begin to collect the same nectar the scout bee had brought back.

When a beehive gets overcrowded and just before a new queen hatches, the old queen and about half of the bees in the hive **swarm**, or leave in a group. After a scout bee has found a hollow log or other suitable place for a new hive, she performs the waggle dance in the middle of the swarm of bees and tells the other bees where it is.

Touch Helps Newborns

Many animal mothers stroke their newborn babies' skin or fur, and some continue to touch their young gently for many days or even years. This assures the young that they will be taken care of. Apes and monkeys carry their young around, and the babies cling to their mothers' fur. Some spiders also carry their young on their backs. The constant bond of touch lets the mother know where her young are, and it keeps them safe.

When a whale mother feels her calf's tongue in one of the two slits near her belly, she squeezes a powerful muscle that squirts milk into its mouth. Lions, tigers, horses, cows, dogs, cats, mice, and many other mammals lick their newborns to show affection and to clean their skin or fur. Baby-sitter bees and ants regularly lick the eggs they care for. This keeps the eggs clean, and by touching the eggs, the baby-sitters show that they care about the young that are growing inside each egg.

Mother sea otters make cooing sounds while brushing their pups' fur with their long claws. Many birds also use their beaks to stroke their young, **preening** or brushing the chicks' feathers. These cleaning gestures also show the parents' affection for their chicks.

When a baby elephant is born in Asia, the mother usually has a female helper who rips open the sack in which the calf lived while it was in its mother's body. Then, to comfort the

The mother chimpanzee communicates to her infant through touch and voice that she will take care of it.

41

young calf, the helper brushes it with her trunk. She also pushes the calf with her trunk, encouraging it to stand up and start walking.

Touch Can Say "I Like You" or "Go Away!"

When two manatees or two groundhogs rub noses or kiss, they greet each other with affection. Animals that play fight by bumping into each other, pushing, pawing, or otherwise playing rough-and-tumble games without trying to hurt each other also communicate that they like each other.

Apes and monkeys show that they care about each other by picking bugs off each other's bodies. They take turns, or they may do it at the same time. Some monkeys also sit in trees with their tails wrapped around each other. Pairs of penguins and many other birds preen each others' feathers, and

These manatees are mated for life, and they show affection by kissing and hugging each other.

some touch bills. Many animals communicate by touch before they mate. Some hug, stroke, or bump into each other, while others chase each other.

Goats butt heads both in play fighting and in real fights, in which one goat tells another to stay away. When two elephant seals fight for a **harem** of cows, each bull knocks his head into the chest of the other. These bulls fight by chest pounding until one gives up and leaves. The winner gets to mate with the harem. Male deer and other animals with horns or antlers use them to defend territory or claim a mate, with the stronger animal pushing the weaker one away.

Live Toothbrushes and Other Cleaning Services

Neon gobies and cleaner wrasses are two of about forty species of small fish that get their food by eating parasites and dead skin off the bodies of parrot fish and other, larger sea animals. While the big "host" fish could easily eat its little cleaners, this rarely happens. Instead, a large fish or eel will show that it wants to be cleaned by taking a certain body position, such as holding still in the water with its head hanging down, or by turning red.

When a host fish wants its teeth cleaned, it opens its mouth wide and several little fish may go in at the same time, removing food remnants and cleaning out sores or wounds that can cause tooth decay or illness. A host fish will also turn over,

A parrot fish waits patiently while two blue-headed wrasses "clean" its skin. The little fish get an easy meal.

open one gill at a time, and otherwise show where it wants to be cleaned.

Some coral beds are "cleaning stations" where cleaner fish and their larger hosts meet regularly. The cleaner fish get food, and the hosts stay healthy. Communicating intent is especially important during these activities because hosts could easily make a meal of the cleaners, which would discourage future cleaning services.

More Living Toothbrushes

Another type of "live toothbrush" may have existed in ancient Egypt. Drawings of the Egyptian plover, or crocodile bird show them picking food remnants from between a crocodile's teeth. While no one really knows if they really cleaned teeth, these birds can be seen riding on a crocodile's back, picking parasites off its skin today.

Vibrations Give Information

Though they lack ears, crabs and other crustaceans pick up vibrations or movements in their environment through tiny hairs on their legs. These messages tell them what kind of animal is making the movements, how large the animal is, and where it is located. When worms dig in the ground, this also causes vibrations and tells moles and other animals where to find them.

A weaver spider catches its prey when it feels it land on its sticky web. The spider quickly runs over and wraps its prey in more sticky silk so it can't escape.

To let her know he wants to mate, a male wolf spider strums a female spider's web as if it were a guitar string.

Animals can communicate with touch even when they can't hear, see, or smell. They can learn things about their environment, comfort or help another animal, find food, or avoid a predator. They can also use touch in play to learn hunting and escape skills.

The male wolf spider cautiously approaches a female on her web after communicating that he only wants to mate and not become her meal.

A fox sniffs the scent of duck as it watches the prey.

Chapter Five

Animals That Miscommunicate

A red fox creeps quietly through tall meadow grass. Suddenly, it smells prey and changes direction. The mother duck sees the fox approaching, but her five ducklings can't fly yet and she can't carry them away to safety. She is determined to save them.

After motioning to her young ones to keep quiet, the duck runs away from the predator. She drags her right wing along the ground while fluttering her left wing. It looks as though she is hurt and can't fly. The fox races after her and gets closer and closer. As soon as they are far enough away from her ducklings, the mother duck flies off.

More Animal Tricks

The prairie warbler is another animal trickster. It will sacrifice itself to save its young. The mother warbler flies to the ground and flaps about, pretending to be hurt. This draws the enemy away from the nest and chicks.

Most animals use false messages to fool predators. A lizard may hide its head by tucking it under its body and then hold its tail up, waving it around as if it were its head. When a predator grabs the tail, the lizard uses a strong muscle to snap it off. The lizard escapes, leaving its enemy with only a small meal. Crabs and lobsters will also cut off one of their own claws or legs to avoid being eaten. While the predator thinks it has caught the whole animal, the crab or lobster scuttles away and hides. These and some other animals can grow a new limb to replace the one that was lost. This usually happens the next time they shed their skin.

Horned lizards, also known as horny toads because of their round bodies, have an unpleasant surprise for their enemies. When caught, they squirt foul-tasting blood from their eyes, as if to say, "This is what you'll get if you eat me!" A predator may wipe its mouth and drop the lizard, which dashes away to safety.

Animals That Are Hard to See

Many animals hide from enemies by using camouflage, making themselves look so much like their environment that they blend into the background and can't be seen. A chameleon is a type of lizard that changes color to match its background. After it has run from one place to another, its skin color will change to match the new surroundings. Squid also change color and blend into their environment. Plaice fish are especially good at matching the environment in which they live. By blending into their environment, these fish are able to hide from predators. An octopus changes color to blend into its background and also squirts black ink to confuse predators.

Deer, rabbits, and many other mammals blend into their surroundings by having darker or lighter fur in summer than in winter. Snowshoe hares, for instance, are relatives of rabbits that turn white in winter. In the spring, after the snow has melted, their fur turns dark again.

Saving Their Young

The broken-wing trick is used by many birds that build their nests and raise their chicks on the ground.

A praying mantis is well hidden by blending with green flower stalks.

A praying mantis looks so much like a twig of the tree it lives on that a predator may not notice it. The three-toed sloth has rows of hair separated by thin grooves in which **algae** or tiny green water plants grow. This makes the sloth's limbs look just like the branches of the trees it lives in.

Camouflage usually happens automatically without the animal thinking about it. While it doesn't always work, camouflage saves many animals from predators. It communicates to the enemy, "there is nothing interesting here."

Other Ways to Fool an Enemy

While camouflage helps animals hide from enemies, it is also used by animals that want to stay hidden while they hunt. Tigers, cougars, snakes, and many other animals blend into their environment while they patiently wait for prey to appear. Many hunters also use the cover of dusk, when it is more difficult for prey to notice them.

The Amazon leaf fish floats on its side near the surface. It looks just like the dead leaves that float nearby in the water. Only when an insect is close enough to grab will the leaf fish move to snap up its meal. While most animals try to keep still until they are ready to pounce on their prey, an ocelot that is after a bird may actually move its tail slightly to draw attention away from its head as it creeps closer but not enough to alert the bird to move away.

A turtle that has been caught by a mother tiger as live prey for her kittens may be able to save itself by playing dead and not moving. If there is no movement, the kittens may get tired of rattling the turtle around and may toss it aside as if it were a stone. Later, the turtle can crawl away unnoticed.

The death's head hawkmoth loves honey. It has the same scent and it can make the same noise as a queen honeybee. By copying the queen bee, this moth has about twenty seconds to steal honey and leave the hive without being found out. If it stays longer, the worker bees will discover its trick and kill it.

Some spiders are so good at copying the zigzag running of ants and using their front legs as if they were antennae that they can actually live with the ants and eat their nest mates. Other spiders have tail ends that look like a wasp's head and spinnerets that look like a wasp's antennae. When they spot a wasp, these spiders can save themselves by walking backward. With their spinnerets held up over their heads, they look just like wasps.

Communicating to Survive

While most animals communicate just what they mean, those that miscommunicate do it to avoid being eaten, to protect

A yellow crab spider is camouflaged on a flower petal where it waits for prey.

their young, or to get food. Animals that blend into their environment have the advantage of being harder to see and catch or of being detected as a hunter. Both camouflage and miscommunication can help animals stay alive longer by fooling their enemies.

Whether animals communicate by sight, sound, smell or touch—or even when they miscommunicate, their signals give other animals many kinds of messages. Those messages can be helpful, such as in sharing a food supply or saving another animal's life, or they may hurt another animal or make it easier to trap. Animals communicate to find a mate, to get food, to protect themselves or their young, and to interact with others of their own species or with other species. Signals can rouse a group of animals to face a common enemy or to flee and hide.

Communication connects animals in many ways. It tells others how and where things are, and it helps get animals what they need to survive.

Glossary

alga—a tiny green water plant

Antarctica—the southernmost part of Earth, which surrounds the South Pole

antenna—a tube on an animal's head that looks like a stick through which it gets information about its environment by detecting vibrations, touch, or smell

blind—a hiding place that allows a person to observe animals without being detected by them

blowhole—the hole on top of a whale's head through which it takes in and blows out air

bond—join together as a pair or group

burrow—a tunnel or hole in the ground made by an animal

camouflage—to become invisible to an enemy by blending into the environment

communicate—to give or receive information from another animal or to have an exchange of information between animals

display—to perform activities that show off strength, beauty, or skill in order to impress another animal

dive-bomb—to fly straight down at high speed

echolocation—the clicking sounds whales, dolphins, and bats send out that bounce off other objects and return, telling these animals where those objects are located, how large they are and if they are moving closer or farther away.

harem—a group of female animals mated to one male

infrasound—sound that some animals can hear but humans can't because it is too low pitched

in heat—a time when an animal has a strong urge to mate and its body is ready to mate

inhibitor—a smell that keeps an animal from doing what it would usually do

miscommunicate—to give a false message or to lie

obedient—willing to obey

pheromone—a chemical message that travels through air or liquid and is picked up as asmell or taste message

photophore—a cell on an animal's body that glows like an electric light

pore—a very tiny opening or hole

predator—an animal that eats another animal

preening—brushing one's own or another animal's fur or feathers

prey—an animal that becomes food for another animal

receptor—a body part that receives messages

rushing ceremony—a custom in which western grebes run across the water in pairs

supersonic sound—sound that can be heard by some animals, but not by humans because it is too high pitched

swarm—honeybees leaving their old hive as a group in order to start a new hive; a large group of bees

swim bladder—a sac filled with air that most bony fish have to help them control the water pressure at different depths in the water

territory—home ground or where an animal lives and usually breeds

vibrating—moving something back and forth or up and down quickly over and over

voice box—the area (usually in the throat) where sound is created by moving vocal cords

waggle dance—a dance performed by a scout honeybee to give worker bees a message about a new food supply or a good location for a new hive

To Find Out More

Books

Benyus, Janine M. *The Secret Language and Remarkable Behavior of Animals*. New York: Black Dog and Leventhal Publishers, 1998.

Resnick, Jane P. *Eyes on Nature—Spiders*. Kidsbooks, Inc., 1996.

Stonehouse, Bernard. *Camouflage*. New York: Tangerine Press, 1999.

Tatham, Betty. *How Animals Play*. Danbury, CT: Franklin Watts, 2004.

Tatham, Betty. *How Animals Shed Their Skin*. Danbury, CT: Franklin Watts, 2002.

Videos

Creatures of the Sea, WBGH Boston Video, 1997.

The Life of Birds, BBC Video, 2002.

Nature: Triumph of Life: Winning Teams, PBS Home Video, 2001.

Organizations and Online Sites

About Marine Mammals
http://nmml.afsc.noaa.gov/education/marinemammals.htm
This is an educational site specializing in the science of marine mammals.

Audubon
http://www.audubon.org/
The Audubon Society's site is perhaps one of the most comprehensive Web sites for information about birds and their environment.

National Geographic Society

http://www.nationalgeographic.com

This site includes more than six thousand plant and animal profiles, videos, audio recordings, and information about worldwide conservation efforts, with interactive maps that lead the user to various regions of the world.

NOVA

http://www.pbs.org/wgbh/nova

This site provides a wide range of information about creatures as well as information on past and future public-television presentations.

Pittsburgh Zoo and PPG Aquarium

http://zoo.pgh.pa.us

This site promotes one of the six major educational zoo and aquarium combinations in the country while providing information about many creatures, endangered species, research, and conservation.

A Note on Sources

Students I consulted about a book on animal communication were very enthusiastic about the subject, so I headed for the library. I couldn't find any book that covered as many different animals as I wanted to write about. I decided that there was a need for *How Animals Communicate*. To write this book, I read many books and articles, and I visited several libraries and looked on the Internet. There was so much information that I had difficulty deciding what to leave out because all animals communicate, and there are so many interesting ways that animals tell each other what they mean. Before sending the manuscript to my editor, I asked my biologist friend Doug Wechsler to review it. Later, my editor had another expert check the manuscript for scientific accuracy.

—*Betty Tatham*

Index

Numbers in *italics* indicate illustrations.

About the Author

Betty Tatham directed three YWCAs for a total of twenty-four years before she retired in 2003 to make writing for children her next career. She wrote the award-winning science book, *Penguin Chick*, which was selected as a Book of the Year by Bank Street College of Education, an Outstanding Science Trade Book by the National Science Teachers Association. For Scholastic Library Publishing, Betty has written several titles for the Watts Library series, including *How Animals Shed Their Skin* and *How Animals Play*. She lives in Holland, Pennsylvannia, with her husband Win.